HIDING IN GRASSLANDS

Deborah Underwood

Heinemann Library
Chicago, Illinois

www.capstonepub.com
Visit our website to find out
more information about
Heinemann-Raintree books.

To order:
☎ Phone 800-747-4992
💻 Visit www.capstonepub.com
to browse our catalog and order online.

Edited by Rebecca Rissman and Nancy Dickmann
Designed by Joanna Hinton Malivoire
Picture research by Tracy Cummins
Originated by Capstone Global Library

Library of Congress Cataloging-in-Publication Data
Underwood, Deborah.
  Hiding in grasslands / Deborah Underwood. -- 1st ed.
    p. cm. -- (Creature camouflage)
  Includes bibliographical references and index.
  ISBN 978-1-4329-4024-9 (hc) -- ISBN 978-1-4329-4033-1
(pb) 1. Grassland animals--Juvenile literature. 2. Camou-
flage (Biology)--Juvenile literature. I. Title.
  QL115.3.U63 2011
  591.47'2--dc22
                                        2009051767

Acknowledgments
The author and publisher are grateful to the following for
permission to reproduce copyright material:
Alamy: Michele Burgess, 25, 26; Ardea: Derrick England,
23, 24; FLPA: David Hosking, 15, 16; Getty Images Inc.:
Andrew Parkinson, 8, Daryl Balfour, 11, 12, Erik Snyder, 27,
Jen and Des Bartlett, 9, Jodi Cobb, Cover, Phil Schermeister,
7; iStockphoto: Kristy Crabtree, 13, 14, Mateusz Cholys, 21,
22; Science Source: Samuel R. Maglione, 19, 20; Shutterstock:
Anna Omelchenko, 6, David P. Smith, 4, Edrich, 17, 18, Eric
Lawton, 10, James Coleman, 28, Jaroslav Machacek, 29,
Liga Alksne, 5.

We would like to thank Michael Bright for his invaluable help
in the preparation of this book.

Every effort has been made to contact copyright holders of
any material reproduced in this book. Any omissions will
be rectified in subsequent printings if notice is given to
the publisher.

All the Internet addresses (URLs) given in this book were
valid at the time of going to press. However, due to the
dynamic nature of the Internet, some addresses may have
changed, or sites may have changed or ceased to exist
since publication. While the author and publisher regret any
inconvenience this may cause readers, no responsibility for
any such changes can be accepted by either the author or
the publisher.

Contents

Some words are printed in bold, **like this**. You can find out what they mean by looking in the glossary.

What Are Grasslands Like?

Grasslands are places where grass is the main type of plant. They can be found in most parts of the world. There are different types of grasslands.

Grasslands called savannas cover much of Africa.

Savannas are grasslands with some trees. They are warm and dry for most of the year. **Prairies** have tall grasses. Their summers are hot, and their winters are cold.

Living in Grasslands

Grassland animals have special **features** that help them **survive** in their surroundings. These features are called **adaptations**.

Zebras may travel hundreds of miles looking for food and water.

Pronghorns can run very quickly. This helps them escape from animals who want to eat them.

An adaptation can be something special about an animal's body. Or it can be something an animal does.

What Is Camouflage?

Camouflage (KAM-uh-flaj) is an **adaptation** that helps animals hide. The color of an animal's skin, fur, or feathers may match the things around it.

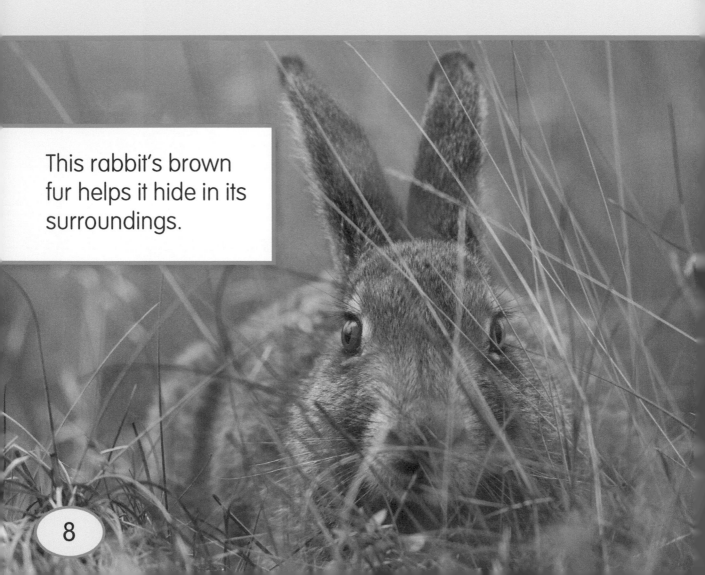

This rabbit's brown fur helps it hide in its surroundings.

This is not a pine cone—it's an animal! The ground pangolin (PANG-guh-lihn) curls up into a ball when in danger.

The shape of an animal may camouflage it, too. So may the things that an animal does, like holding very still when danger is near. Why do you think animals need to hide?

Coyotes often sneak up on their prey. The color of their coats helps them to hide.

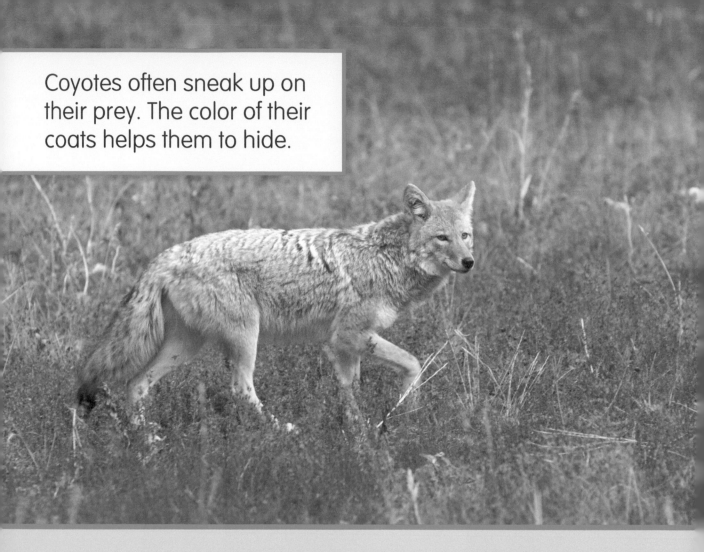

Animals that eat other animals are called **predators**. **Camouflage** helps them catch food. Animals that predators eat are called **prey**. Camouflage helps prey animals hide from predators!

Find the Grassland Animals

Lion

It isn't easy to spot lions in tall **savanna** grasslands. The color of their fur helps them hide in the dry grass. This lets them sneak up on prey.

CAMOUFLAGED

Adult lions have few **predators**. But leopards and hyenas may hunt lion cubs. The cubs' coats have brown spots. The spots **blend in** with the ground.

REVEALED

Rattlesnake

Rattlesnakes have dark spots on their backs. They hunt small animals. Their **camouflage** helps them blend in. They can sneak up on **prey**.

Rattlesnakes have a **venomous** bite. But some birds eat rattlesnakes. A rattlesnake's **camouflage** can help it hide from a **predator**.

REVEALED

CAMOUFLAGED

Burrowing owl

Burrowing owls are only eight or nine inches tall. They sleep in underground homes called **burrows**. The color of the owls' feathers helps them hide from predators.

When an owl comes out of its **burrow**, it may stand nearby. It may perch on a branch. Its **camouflage** lets it **blend in** with soil or branches.

REVEALED

Giraffe

It might seem like a giraffe would stand out anywhere! But a giraffe's brown spots help it to hide. It can be hard to see a giraffe standing among trees and bushes.

CAMOUFLAGED

The shape of its long neck can also **camouflage** a giraffe. Its neck can look like a tree trunk!

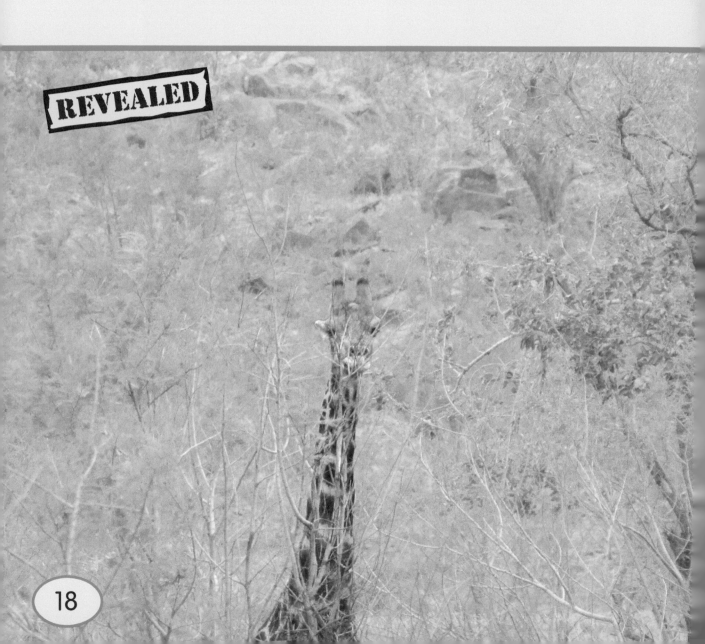

REVEALED

CAMOUFLAGED

Savanna monitor

The savanna monitor is a lizard that lives in Africa. The **patterns** and colors on the lizard's skin help to camouflage it in dry grasses and soil.

Savanna monitors can grow to be about five feet long. Their **camouflage** helps them hide from **predators**, such as snakes and birds.

REVEALED

Grasshopper

This grasshopper's green and brown colors make it look like grass. A hungry bird might have a hard time seeing it!

Grasshoppers are good jumpers, but most can't fly. They need their **camouflage** to help them stay safe from **predators**.

REVEALED

CAMOUFLAGED

Great bustard

A female great bustard (BUS-tuhrd) lays eggs on the ground. The colors of her feathers help to camouflage her as she sits on her nest.

Great bustard chicks are gray with dark markings. Foxes, crows, and badgers may eat the chicks. The chicks' **camouflage** makes it hard for **predators** to see them.

REVEALED

Cheetah

A cheetah's light yellow fur is covered with small black spots. The spots make the cheetah almost disappear in grasses. This helps the cheetah sneak up on **prey**.

Cheetah cubs have long, gray fur on their backs and heads. This color **blends in** with **savanna** grasses. It helps hide the cubs from lions and other **predators**.

REVEALED

Prairie dogs' brown fur helps them blend in with dirt and grass.

A cheetah's spotted coat helps it hunt. A grasshopper's green body helps it hide. Grassland animals would have a hard time **surviving** without **camouflage**!

Animals that Stand Out

Some grassland animals do not hide. Skunks make a bad smell when they are scared. Their black-and-white fur warns other animals to stay away.

An animal that scares a skunk will get a smelly surprise!

Bumblebees give painful stings to animals that bother them.

A bumblebee's stripes also warn other animals to stay away. An animal that gets too close to a bumblebee might get stung!

Glossary

adaptation special feature that helps an animal survive in its surroundings

blend in matches well with the things around it

burrow animal's underground home

camouflage adaptation that helps an animal blend in

feature special part of an animal

pattern shapes and marks on an animal's skin, fur, or feathers

prairie grasslands with tall grasses, hot summers, and cold winters

predator animal that eats other animals

prey animal that other animals eat

savanna warm or hot grasslands with scattered trees

survive stay alive

venomous something dangerous that can make you sick, or even kill you

Find Out More

Books to read

Dunphy, Madeleine, and Tom Leonard (illustrator). *Here is the African Savanna*. Berkeley, CA: Web of Life Children's Books, 2006.

Johnson, Rebecca L., and Phyllis V. Saroff (illustrator). *A Walk in the Prairie*. Minneapolis, MN: Carolrhoda Books, 2001.

Patent, Dorothy Hinshaw, and William Muñoz (illustrator). *Life in a Grassland*. Minneapolis, MN: Lerner Publications, 2002.

Websites

www.defenders.org/wildlife_and_habitat/habitat/grasslands.php
Defenders of Wildlife grasslands habitat information

www.mbgnet.net/grasslnd/index.htm
Missouri Botanical Garden grasslands information

Index